SUMMARY OF MORALITY:

Restoring the Common Good in Divided Times
By

Jonathan Sacks
BlinkRead

BlinkRead

Copyright(c) 2020

Table of Content

SYNOPSIS:

Morality (2020) is a detailed deconstruction of our current social climate and a lucid account of how we got here. Part intellectual history and part manifesto of moral truths, this thoughtful work uncovers the roots of the rifts in contemporary society and points out a path toward a more just future.

ABOUT AUTHOR:

Rabbi Jonathan Sacks is a best-selling author of more than 30 books including Not in God's Name: Confronting Religious Violence (2015) and The Great Partnership: God, Science and the Search for Meaning (2012). He is the former Chief Rabbi of the United Hebrew Congregations of the Commonwealth and has lectured on spirituality and morality at dozens of leading religious institutions around the world.

DISCLAIMER:

This book is a SUMMARY. It is meant to be a companion, not a replacement, to the original book. Please note that this summary is not authorized, licensed, approved, or endorsed by the author or publisher of the main book. The author of this summary is wholly responsible for the content of this summary and is not associated with the original author or publisher of the main book.

WHAT'S IN IT FOR ME? AN EPIDEMIC HANDBOOK.

The world around us seems more turbulent and tumultuous than ever. In these times of rapid change, society has cast aside traditional values and it's unclear what could – or should – come to replace them.

With Morality: Restoring the Common Good in Divided Times, Rabbi Jonathan Sacks contemplates how we got here and how we can move forward without leaving anyone behind. Drawing on decades of scholarly study and spiritual reflection, Sacks traces the roots of our current crises from the ancient Greeks to today.

In this book-in-blinks, you'll discover the ways in which the concept of morality has shaped society through the ages, and why it should still be a central concern. By taking lessons from the past and applying them to contemporary conflicts, Sacks illuminates the importance of cultivating a strong moral foundation, both as individuals and as a community.

In these blinks, you'll learn

what cows, chickens, and grass can tell us about moral codes;
why social media makes us mean; and
how science can solve problems but let us down.

SOCIETY'S EMPHASIS ON INDIVIDUALITY LEAVES US ISOLATED AND VULNERABLE.

Beethoven, Bach, Brahms. All of these men devoted their entire lives to composing symphonies. With their intense dedication and powerful talents, they penned some of the most beautiful orchestral music in history. Yet without the orchestra, we would never have heard it.

The fact is, even a genius can't bring a symphony to life on his own. It takes the teamwork and coordination of dozens of musicians all working together. Without this community effort, all grand symphonies would be reduced to rather lonely solos.

The key message here is: Society's emphasis on individuality leaves us isolated and vulnerable.

For the past few decades, society has become increasingly focused on the individual. This shift is reflected all over our culture, even in our pop music. A study from the University of Kentucky found that since 1980, hit songs have included fewer lyrics about "we" and "us" and more about "me" and "I."

But that's just a small example. Our lifestyles have changed, too. These days, people live more solitary lives. They marry later, have fewer children, and join fewer social groups than in the past. In the United States, the percentage of people living alone has doubled in just 50 years. In large cities, nearly half of all people live on their own.

This shift toward individuality has left us lonelier, which can have dire consequences. For one, chronic loneliness has serious health implications. Research has linked feeling alone to higher stress levels and reduced immune system response. One study even found that long-term loneliness is as harmful to health as smoking 15 cigarettes a day.

Our obsession with individualism has also boosted the self-help industry. Each year, thousands of books are published that claim we can fix our problems by focusing on ourselves. But this narcissistic impulse only leaves us more lonely and disconnected.

A better way for us to improve our lives is to act in service to others. You can do this by stepping outside yourself and evaluating your behavior from an outsider's perspective. Rather than basing your actions and decisions around your immediate needs and desires, reflect on how others may experience your actions.

Such an approach to life values the collective "us" over the individual "I." This process is sometimes called "unselfing" and is the basis of morality. In the next blinks, we'll delve deeper into why this process can be so difficult.

NEW NORMS GOVERNING RELATIONSHIPS DISCOURAGE US FROM ACTING MORALLY.

Take a scroll through your Facebook, Instagram, or Snapchat feed. How many friends and connections do you have? According to a 2018 study, if you're like the average British adult, it's probably around 500. Now, how many of those connections could you rely on in an emergency?

Unfortunately, that number is probably much lower. In fact, that same study showed the average adult only has five "true friends" – that is, friends who would make some sort of sacrifice for them. Those other online friends are just not the same.

The key message here is: New norms governing relationships discourage us from acting morally.

It's hard to understate the reach and impact of social media. In 2019, more than six billion people were using internet-connected devices around the world. Of those, more than two billion were active users of Facebook. When you include other forms of social media, that number jumps even higher.

Now, all this networking has a lot of potential for good. It's wonderful that people can keep in touch with loved ones and access all sorts of information. However, it has a downside, too. The average teenager now spends seven to nine hours on electronic devices every day. And as the amount of time people spend in front of a screen rises, the amount of time they spend interacting face-to-face declines.

All this screen time creates problems. For one, social media is bad for building full, well-rounded relationships. Online, people tend to show only their best sides and to interact only on a superficial level. Such relationships can feel more like transactions than mutually supportive encounters.

This way of interacting can lead to weaker social bonds that make it more difficult for us to think selflessly. A recent study from the University of California even found that increased use of social media correlated with lower levels of empathy and higher levels of depression.

Adding to this, family structure has also changed drastically. Since the 1960s, the marriage rate has declined significantly in many countries. In 1968, 56 percent of Americans under 30 were married. Today, that number is closer to 23 percent. To Sacks, this is a problem. He asserts that traditional marriage is a valuable social institution that promotes important values like mutual support and responsibility.

So as people rely less on traditional family structures and have fewer face-to-face interactions, thinking outside of the self becomes difficult. We'll explore the consequences of this shift in the next blink.

IN ECONOMICS, SELF-INTEREST SHOULD ALWAYS BE TEMPERED BY MORAL CONSCIENCE.

It inspired the beautiful portraits of Renaissance Italy. It informed the passionate writings of Kirkegaard, Voltaire, and Kant. It fueled the entrepreneurial spirit of early America. And, in 2008, it crashed the entire world economy.

Our relationship with the ethos of individualism has never been static. It's been growing and changing for centuries, influencing everything from our art and culture to our politics and economics. Sometimes, these changes are good. Other times, they're disastrous.

The key message here is: In economics, self-interest should always be tempered by moral conscience.

Our current free-market economy has done amazing things. In the past century, it has raised millions of people from poverty, produced innumerable consumer goods, and generally enhanced our overall quality of life. Our individualism is partially responsible for this success. People learn new skills, create new products, and start businesses – all in the name of self-interest.

However, this system only works when people also recognize the needs of others. Otherwise, things get messy. Just consider the 2008 financial crisis. This man-made disaster kicked off when banks and other companies created financial products they knew were unstable. Since they were confident they could profit even if many people suffered, they sold them anyway. As a result, a select few became rich, while millions of people in the United States and in Britain lost their homes.

This type of greed, unrestrained by moral codes, erodes the trust and cooperation needed to have a functioning society. This is especially concerning when it comes to our pursuit of happiness. For much of history, happiness came from doing good. Even early philosophers such as Aristotle claimed true happiness, or eudaemonia, came from living a virtuous life.

Now, however, happiness is equated simply with feeling good. It's about experiencing pleasant sensations and has no moral dimension. This is a dangerous idea because it leads individuals and businesses alike to seek short-term satisfaction — that is, pleasure or profit — rather than higher goals such as fairness or justice.

On a personal level, we can avoid this trap by being more mindful of where our happiness comes from. Contrast the brief joy of acquiring a new material item with the deep satisfaction that comes from sustaining a meaningful friendship. Obviously, the latter will bring you more contentment over time. Cast in these terms, the pursuit of happiness can also be a deeply moral endeavor.

A STABLE SOCIETY REQUIRES A SHARED MORAL CODE.

Check the news. You'll see stories of riots, terrorism, and political oppression. Pop into your local bookstore. You'll see bestsellers with titles like How Democracy Ends, Why Liberalism Failed, and The Strange Death of Europe.

It seems that no matter where you look, things appear bleak. So how did we get here? To find the answer, we might need to look in a mirror. The way we see ourselves and our place in society might be the issue.

The key message here is: A stable society requires a shared moral code.

For centuries, philosophers have debated the role of the state in society. One group, made up of thinkers like John Locke, argued that individuals were born with certain rights. Thus, the state should exist to protect individual liberty. Another group, headed by Jean-Jacques Rousseau, argued that rights were conferred by the state, so the state must provide for the "common good."

In recent decades, Rousseau's argument has won. People now expect the state to deliver all sorts of common "goods" that used to be provided by individuals, families, and communities. This includes everything from financial security to personal happiness.

Of course, often, the state cannot provide these things. Thus, people are left disappointed, angry, and scared. They lose faith in traditional politics and political figures. For example, a 2018 survey found that only 18 percent of British people trust their political parties. As a result of this distrust, people may seek answers from more authoritarian leaders or dangerous populist movements.

Further fueling these tensions is the rise of so-called "identity politics." For Sacks, identity politics are ideologies that encourage people to link their personal value strongly to certain demographic categories such as race, gender, or sexual orientation. Such an ideology emphasizes personal differences over common similarities. It emphasizes the "I" over the "we" and creates conflict where there could be cooperation.

One way to stem this tide of turmoil is to take a cue from religion. Many faiths, such as Judaism, have long, stable histories because they teach the importance of maintaining shared moral codes and traditions. The faithful are encouraged to find solace in each other, not in the government or the latest populist fad.

According to Sacks, many of today's problems have their roots in the 1960s, when countercultural movements cast aside traditional values in favor of personal expression, social experimentation, and drugs. If society, like religion, had taken a more conservative approach to change, some of today's troubles might have been avoided.

TO SUSTAIN A MORAL COMMUNITY, WE MUST RESPECT THE TRUTH.

It's the year 1274 BCE. Ramesses II returns to Egypt after fighting the Hittites in the city of Kadesh. He tells the Egyptians to celebrate, for they won the battle. Back in Kadesh, the Hittites are also celebrating. Their leader is also claiming victory.

Who really won? We still don't know. Certainty could be hard to come by in ancient Egypt. Today, it's even harder. Unscrupulous politicians, biased news organizations, and social media make spreading misinformation easier than ever. However, that doesn't mean we should give up on the truth.

The key message here is: To sustain a moral community, we must respect the truth.

Lies and deceit are as old as the pyramids, but in the contemporary world, the truth seems more scarce than ever. Some writers even call this the post-truth era. Consider the 2016 presidential race. This event was marred by huge amounts of misinformation on social media. And to many, it didn't matter. Emotions and personal beliefs were more important than objective facts.

For Sacks, this problem can be traced back to the ascendance of postmodernist philosophy. This framework favors a fluid conception of reality with no objective truth. Texts have no true meaning, only interpretations. There's no real history, only subjective narratives. Seeing the world this way is dangerous, because it undermines the concept of shared beliefs, values, and morals necessary for society to function.

Traditionally, we relied on universities to produce the shared truths that guide society.

However, these too have been undermined. Rather than hosting healthy debates and open dialogues, universities are increasingly treated as "safe spaces." Students fight to limit who can speak on campus and harshly condemn any language that might be offensive.

While such actions might be well-intended, excluding any controversial belief from classrooms stifles the free exchange of ideas necessary for pursuing higher truths. Of course, sometimes seeking truth will lead to conflict. Still, disagreements can actually be beneficial – if done correctly.

Judaism offers a concept called "argument for the sake of heaven." In these arguments, both sides respect each other's beliefs, values, and intellect. There is no censorship or lecturing. Instead, each party is careful to both speak and listen. The goal is not to claim victory, but to find the truth.

Sometimes finding the truth means acknowledging uncomfortable facts or unexpected ambiguities. However, a society that values truth can build trust and share a stronger moral framework.

BUILDING A MORAL COMMUNITY MEANS LOOKING FORWARD, NOT BACK.

Yisrael Kristal lost everything in the Holocaust. He lost his health, his business, and his entire family. Yet, after leaving Auschwitz, he kept going. He moved to Israel, started a successful candy company, and, at 113 years old, he became the oldest person ever to have a bar mitzvah.

Like many Holocaust survivors, Kristal didn't let victimhood define him. While he suffered incredible personal anguish, he left it in the past by concentrating on building a better future. If we want a moral society, we should follow his lead.

The key message here is: Building a moral community means looking forward, not back.

Human society has never been perfect. At times, those in power have harmed and oppressed individuals, groups, and entire communities. Correcting these wrongs isn't easy but it is moral. However, it is important to ensure that our actions are about creating a better future, not simply condemning the past.

Unfortunately, our current culture doesn't always meet this standard. One major way we are failing is with the resurgence of public shaming. This is an old phenomenon that has acquired new strength in the age of social media. You've probably seen it happen yourself. Someone makes a mistake, like making a rude joke or stating a controversial opinion, and suddenly a whole mob of voices rises to shout them down.

This form of vigilante justice has an appeal. It can help traditionally powerless groups call out serious bad actors. Yet there are risks.

For one, it does away with due process. The accused has no chance to plead her case and may be wrongly condemned. Additionally, the punishment is doled out from a place of anger. True justice can only come from an impartial, outside source, not an unruly mob.

If we want a moral society, we must temper our more aggressive instincts. When you are wronged, it's tempting to seek revenge. You may want to respond to one hurtful act with another. However, this only perpetuates a cycle of pain. Instead, we must learn to forgive. We must offer our adversaries a chance to repent and rectify their wrongs.

This may seem difficult, especially as society becomes more polarized and combative. Still, maintaining civility – that is, approaching each other with kindness and respect – is essential for building a moral future that leaves no one behind. In the next blink, we'll start looking at just what this moral future could look like.

MORALITY COMES FROM OUR ABILITY TO MAKE CHOICES AND MAKE MEANING.

In the beginning, Earth was the center of the universe, and humankind was the masterful creation of God. Then along came Copernicus and Darwin. Suddenly, the Earth was just another planet, and humans just another animal.

Quite the downgrade, right? While scientific advancement has many benefits, it also changes how we see ourselves. Yet as we learn more about how the world works, it's important to remember what makes humans special.

The key message here is: Morality comes from our ability to make choices and make meaning.

Many modern strains of thought describe the world in a detached, impersonal way. Evolution tells us that humanity emerged from natural selection, that we are just the result of millions of years of random chance. Freud's psychoanalytic theories teach us that we are all driven by innate, unconscious drives. And Marxism argues that our actions are compelled by historic economic forces.

These empirical frameworks are useful in some analytical contexts; however, they don't tell the whole story. They describe the world in deterministic terms, so they leave out an important aspect of the human experience: free will.

Jewish and Christian traditions teach that humans are not mere machines controlled by outside forces. We are conscious agents. We are free to evaluate the world around us and make decisions about how to behave. This freedom to think and act sets us apart from the natural world. It is the basis of human dignity.

Being free, conscious agents comes with a responsibility. We must make sense of the world. We have to decide which values to cherish, which principles are important, and which aspirations are worthy. In short, we have to make meaning.

This leads us to a moral choice: Do we create our own, individual meanings, or do we create shared, communal meanings? The first option means living in a world dominated by the "I." Only your wants and desires matter and no one else's. The second option, shared meanings, creates a world of the "we." In this world, people can step outside themselves. They can set aside their own immediate desires for the greater good.

Creating shared meanings allows us to build a shared moral code. When we share a moral code, we can build communities based on trust, cooperation, and mutual respect. Without such cohesion, society will descend into chaos. So which moral code is the right one? We'll answer that question in the next blink.

WHILE THERE ARE MANY MORAL CODES, IT'S IMPORTANT TO COMMIT TO ONE OF THEM.

Here's an experiment: show a child a picture of three things – a cow, a chicken, and some grass. Then ask them which two things go together. The answer is obvious, right? Well, that depends on whom you ask.

Researchers who conducted this experiment found that answers varied. American children were likely to group the cow with the chicken. In contrast, Chinese children often paired the cow and the grass. This exercise shows that the physical world can be seen through multiple lenses. And when it comes to morality, the same principle applies.

Here's the key message: While there are many moral codes, it's important to commit to one of them.

Humanity is extremely diverse. We live in a world with more than six thousand languages, hundreds of religions, and innumerable different cultures and subcultures. Unsurprisingly, there's a diversity of moral codes as well. What may be right and appropriate for some people in some places might be wrong and offensive to people in others.

One way to make sense of all this variation is with the concept of thick and thin moral codes. Thin moral codes are abstract principles that apply across cultures. These include basic ideas like "Don't harm each other." On the other hand, thick moral codes are specific, detailed rules that apply to contexts and cultures. These are the rituals, taboos, and social norms that make cultures different from one another.

Because thick moral codes are culturally specific, they can be very different. For instance, the moral code of ancient Athens was focused on the virtues of serving the polis and acting with courage in battle. Meanwhile, the moral code of China is highly influenced by the teachings of Confucius and stresses piety and respect for elders.

For Sacks, it's important to understand and respect different codes, but it's also important to commit to one for yourself and share it with a community. Committing to a moral code is a bit like speaking a language; it works best when you know one very well and can speak it often with others.

Traditionally, the communal nature of religion has been an effective way to spread moral codes across large populations. In many societies, a shared religion is the basis for large-scale cooperation that would otherwise be difficult to coordinate. For example, in Bali, rituals connected to the worship of a water deity help communities manage the complex irrigation systems necessary to grow rice.

In the West, organized religion is on the decline. In the next blink, we'll examine what that means for the future of our moral codes.

WE CAN REINVIGORATE SOCIETY'S MORAL CODE BY WORKING TOGETHER.

September 11, 2001, was an unusual day for everyone. But it was especially strange for Gander, Newfoundland. As aircraft all over North America were forced to land, more than thirty airliners filled with passengers ended up in this small, isolated community in Canada.

The people of Gander rose to the occasion. They provided food, housing, and warm compassion to seven thousand strangers stranded in their town. On one of the darkest days in history, they showed that humanity was still basically good.

Here's the key message: We can reinvigorate society's moral code by working together.

It is easy to be pessimistic about the fate of the world. Our current cultural climate seems to be defined by fear, anger, and isolation. The supremacy of the market has turned much of society into an endless competition for profit. Meanwhile, the retreat of the state has left many with fewer social services and legal protections than previous generations had.

Clearly, we cannot wait for the market or the state to change the course of history. We must take that responsibility ourselves. This may sound like a daunting task. However, it can be accomplished with one act of kindness at a time. Reaching out and taking care of those around you is the first step towards larger change.

When Sacks was a young rabbi, he had to perform many funerals. Before each one, he asked the friends and family of the deceased what their loved ones should be remembered for. Without fail, they always responded in the same way. They recalled the positive acts the departed had carried out, the care they gave their families, and the role they played in the community.

If we want the future to be moral, we must also focus on what we can do for each other. We must shift our society from a mindset of "I" to a mindset of "we." Sacks calls this the "politics of covenant." When we build a covenant with others, we reaffirm our mutual responsibility to each other's well-being. In this new framework, individuals, businesses, and communities should concentrate less on self-interest and more on cooperation.

Establishing a world based on covenants is not easy, but it is possible. This politics of mutual responsibility has done great things in the past, such as ending slavery or eradicating disease, and it can happen again.

It simply requires people to care for one another and commit to that belief.

FINAL SUMMARY.

The key message in these blinks:

When life spins out of control and relationships feel unmanageable, it's often because there's a lack of boundaries. Boundaries empower us to own and address our own problems, desires, and feelings. They help us support others in their problems without shouldering their burdens, and enable us to ask for and accept help. Boundaries aren't just necessary; they can be a source of love and joy in our lives.

Actionable advice:

Form a boundary support group.

It takes a lot of strength to identify, create, and maintain boundaries in your life. Ever heard the saying "strength in numbers?"

Form a boundary support group, where you can flex those boundary-setting muscles in safety. Discuss boundary-related successes and failures, and even test boundary-setting out on each other.

BLINKREAD

BlinkRead is dedicated to creating high-quality summaries of non-fiction books to help you through the bestseller list each week

We cover books in self-help, business, personal development, science & technology, health & fitness, history, and memoir/biography. Our books are expertly written and professionally edited to provide top-notch content. We're here to help you decide which books to invest your time and money reading.

Absorb everything you need to know in 20 minutes or less!

We release new summaries each and every week, so join our mailing list to stay up-to-date and get free summaries right in your inbox!

CPSIA information can be obtained
at www.ICGtesting.com
Printed in the USA
BVHW041636201120
593826BV00009B/454

ISBN 9798680236697

Dontrell, Who Kissed the Sea

by Nathan Alan Davis

SAMUEL FRENCH